WRAPS for every wear

Wrap up accessories that are so feminine — and so fun to knit!

Meet Jeannine LaRoche

Jeannine LaRoche once owned a yarn and needlecraft shop. When her customers weren't able to find a pattern that met their needs, Jeannine would design one for them. Her creations caught the attention of a yarn salesman, and after meeting with a vice president of the company, she entered the world of fashion design.

Since those early days, Jeannine's work has appeared in numerous instruction books and national magazines. She has also been featured on TV and radio programs in the Boston, Massachusetts area. Although Jeannine closed her shop years ago, she continues teaching classes in local schools and church groups.

While working on this collection of shawls, stoles, and ponchos, Jeannine went on a cruise, taking some of her designs with her. The passengers seated at her dinner table looked forward to seeing the different wraps she wore each evening.

Jeannine says, "I would like to encourage everyone, young and old, to use their God-given talents to bless others. At 85 years of age, I still teach four classes a week, and students often drop in for extra help. Last year, I moved to Florida and drove my little lime green Volkswagen Beetle (with a moon roof) all the way from California! Life is a challenge—enjoy it!"

For more of Jeannine's exciting knit designs, get your copies of #4577 Knit Lace & Leaves for Baby *and #4453* Knit Hoodies for Kids *at LeisureArts.com.*

*W*ant to refresh your look? You could buy a new pair of shoes. Or wear your hair a different way. Or you could knit an amazing new wrap! This collection of seven sensational shawls, stoles, and ponchos offers a special accessory for every mood and occasion. Toss the stoles around your shoulders or just wear them tucked around your arms. The ponchos are versatile, too—you can align them parallel to your shoulders, or position them on point. So whether you're dressed in jeans and boots, skirt and heels, or pants and flats, you'll find the perfect wrap—*for every wear!*

LEISURE ARTS, INC.
Little Rock, Arkansas

feather & fan stole

Finished Size: 15" wide x 70" long
(38 x 178 cm)

MATERIALS
Fine Weight Yarn
9 ounces, 255 grams
29" (73.5 cm) Circular knitting needle,
size 8 (5 mm) **or** size needed for gauge

GAUGE: In pattern,
one repeat (18 sts) = 3" (7.5 cm)

Techniques used:
- Knit increase *(Figs. 1a & b, page 19)*
- YO *(Fig. 3, page 19)*
- K2 tog *(Fig. 5, page 19)*

BODY
Cast on 72 sts.

Row 1: Knit across.

Row 2 (Increase row)**:** (Knit increase, K3)
across: 90 sts.

Row 3: Knit across.

Row 4 (Right side)**:** K2 tog 3 times, (YO, K1)
6 times ★ K2 tog 6 times, (YO, K1) 6 times;
repeat from ★ across to last 6 sts,
K2 tog 3 times.

Rows 5-7: Knit across.

Repeat Rows 4-7 for pattern until piece
measures approximately 69^3/$_4$" (177 cm) from
cast on edge **or** to desired length, ending by
working Row 5.

Decrease Row: (K2 tog, K3) across: 72 sts.

Last Row: Knit across.

Bind off all sts in **knit**.

open work cover-up

INTERMEDIATE

Finished Size: 54" (137 cm) around bottom
edge x 13" long (33 cm)
excluding fringe

MATERIALS

Medium Weight Yarn
6 ounces, 170 grams
29" (73.5 cm) Circular knitting needle,
size 10¹/₂ (6.5 mm) **or** size needed for gauge
Marker
Crochet hook (for fringe)

GAUGE: In pattern,
17 sts and 20 rnds = 4¹/₂" (11.5 cm)

Techniques used:
* Invisible increase *(Fig. 2, page 19)*
* YO *(Fig. 3, page 19)*
* K2 tog *(Fig. 5, page 19)*

BODY

Beginning at neck edge, cast on 72 sts; place
a marker to indicate beginning of round
(see Markers, page 20).

Rnds 1-5: (K1, P1) around.

Rnd 6: (K6, invisible increase) around: 84 sts.

Rnd 7: Knit around.

Rnd 8: (K7, invisible increase) around: 96 sts.

Rnd 9 (Increase row)**:** (YO twice, K2 tog)
around: 144 sts.

Rnd 10: K1, drop second YO, (K2, drop second
YO) around to last st, K1: 96 sts.

Rnd 11: (K8, invisible increase) around: 108 sts.

Rnd 12: Knit around.

Rnd 13: (K9, invisible increase) around: 120 sts.

Rnds 14 and 15: Repeat Rnds 9 and 10.

Rnd 16: (K 10, invisible increase) around: 132 sts.

Rnd 17: Knit around.

Rnd 18: (K 11, invisible increase) around: 144 sts.

Rnds 19 and 20: Repeat Rnds 9 and 10.

Rnd 21: (K 12, invisible increase) around: 156 sts.

Rnd 22: Knit around.

Rnd 23: (K 13, invisible increase) around: 168 sts.

Rnds 24 and 25: Repeat Rnds 9 and 10.

Rnd 26: (K 14, invisible increase) around: 180 sts.

Rnds 27 and 28: Knit around.

Rnds 29 and 30: Repeat Rnds 9 and 10.

Rnd 31: (K 15, invisible increase) around: 192 sts.

Rnds 32 and 33: Knit around.

Rnds 34 and 35: Repeat Rnds 9 and 10.

Rnd 36: (K 16, invisible increase) around: 204 sts.

Rnds 37 and 38: Knit around.

Rnd 39 (Increase row)**:** (YO twice, K2 tog) around: 306 sts.

Rnd 40: K1, drop second YO, (K2, drop second YO) around to last st, K1: 204 sts.

Rnds 41-43: Knit around.

Repeat Rnds 39-43 until Body measures approximately 13" (33 cm) from cast on edge **or** to desired length, ending by working Rnd 43.

Bind off all sts in **knit**.

FRINGE

Holding 2 strands of yarn together, each 10" (25.5 cm) long, add Fringe to Body, spacing as desired *(Figs. 8a & b, page 20)*.

triangle
cover-up

Finished Size: 43" wide x 12" long
(109 x 30.5 cm)
excluding fringe

MATERIALS
Light Weight Yarn
6 ounces, 170 grams
29" (73.5 cm) Circular knitting needle,
size 8 (5 mm) **or** size needed for gauge
Yarn needle
Crochet hook (for fringe)

GAUGE: In pattern,
12 sts and 20 rows = 4" (10 cm)

Techniques used:
*   Knit increase *(Figs. 1a & b, page 19)*
*   YO *(Fig. 3, page 19)*

BODY (Make 2)
Beginning at bottom, cast on 11 sts **loosely**.

Work first and last 3 sts of each row more loosely to prevent the edge from binding on the finished piece.

Rows 1 and 2: Knit across.

Row 3 (Right side - Increase row)**:** K2, knit increase, YO, (K1, YO) across to last 3 sts, knit increase, K2: 19 sts.

Row 4 (Decrease row)**:** K2, knit increase, (K1, drop YO) across to last 4 sts, K1, knit increase, K2: 15 sts.

Rows 5 and 6 (Increase rows)**:** K2, knit increase, knit across to last 3 sts, knit increase, K2: 19 sts.

Rows 7-61: Repeat Rows 3-6, 13 times; then repeat Rows 3-5 once **more**: 129 sts.

Row 62: Knit across.

Bind off all sts in **knit**, leaving a long end for sewing.

FINISHING
Thread needle with long end. With **right** sides together, sew bound off edges of both pieces together to form shoulders, leaving a 9$\frac{1}{2}$" (24 cm) neck opening in center.

FRINGE
Holding 2 strands of yarn together, each 8" (20.5 cm) long, add fringe to Body, spacing as desired *(Figs. 8a & b, page 20)*.

zig zag stole

Finished Size: 17¹/₂" wide x 60" long
(44.5 x 152.5 cm)

MATERIALS

Light Weight Yarn
11 ounces, 312 grams
29" (73.5 cm) Circular knitting needle,
size 8 (5 mm) **or** size needed for gauge

GAUGE: In pattern,
20 sts and 19 rows = 4" (10 cm)

Techniques used:
- Knit increase (Figs. 1a & b, page 19)
- YO (Fig. 3, page 19)
- K2 tog (Fig. 5, page 19)

BODY

Cast on 71 sts.

Row 1: K3, (knit increase, K3) across: 88 sts.

Row 2 AND ALL WRONG SIDE ROWS: Knit across.

Row 3 (Right side)**:** K3, K2 tog, (YO, K2, K2 tog) across to last 3 sts, YO, K3.

Row 5: K2, K2 tog, (YO, K2, K2 tog) across to last 4 sts, YO, K4.

Row 7: K5, K2 tog, (YO, K2, K2 tog) across to last 5 sts, YO, K5.

Row 9: K4, K2 tog, (YO, K2, K2 tog) across to last 6 sts, YO, K6.

Row 11: K3, K2 tog, (YO, K2, K2 tog) across to last 3 sts, YO, K3.

Row 13: K5, YO, K2 tog, (K2, YO, K2 tog) across to last 5 sts, K5.

Row 15: K6, YO, K2 tog, (K2, YO, K2 tog) across to last 4 sts, K4.

Row 17: K3, YO, K2 tog, (K2, YO, K2 tog) across to last 3 sts, K3.

Row 19: K4, YO, K2 tog, (K2, YO, K2 tog) across to last 2 sts, K2.

Repeat Rows 2-19 for pattern until piece measures approximately 60" (152.5 cm) from cast on edge **or** to desired length, ending by working a **knit** row.

Last Row: K3, (K2 tog, K3) across: 71 sts.

Bind off all sts in **knit.**

leaf shawl

 EASY +

Finished Size: 56" wide x 29" long
(142 x 73.5 cm) excluding fringe

MATERIALS
Fine Weight Yarn
6 ounces, 170 grams
Super Fine Weight Yarn
3.5 ounces, 100 grams
29" (73.5 cm) Circular knitting needle,
size 8 (5 mm) **or** size needed for gauge
Crochet hook (for fringe)

GAUGE: In pattern,
20 sts and 24 rows = 5" (12.75 cm)

Techniques used:
- YO *(Fig. 3, page 19)*
- K2 tog *(Fig. 5, page 19)*
- Slip 1 as if to knit, K2 tog, PSSO *(Figs. 6a & b, page 20)*

BODY
Holding 2 strands of super fine weight yarn and one strand of fine weight yarn together, cast on 4 sts.

Rows 1 and 2: Knit across.

Row 3 (Right side)**:** K2, YO, K2: 5 sts.

Row 4: K2, P1, K2.

Row 5: K2, YO, K1, YO, K2: 7 sts.

Row 6: K2, P3, K2.

Row 7: K2, YO, K3, YO, K2: 9 sts.

Row 8 AND ALL WRONG SIDE ROWS: K2, purl across to last 2 sts, K2.

Row 9: K2, YO, K5, YO, K2: 11 sts.

Row 11: K2, YO, K7, YO, K2: 13 sts.

Row 13: K2, YO, K9, YO, K2: 15 sts.

Row 15: K2, YO, K1, YO, K3, slip 1 as if to knit, K2 tog, PSSO, K3, YO, K1, YO, K2: 17 sts.

Instructions continued on page 12.

Row 17: K2, YO, K3, YO, K2, slip 1 as if to knit, K2 tog, PSSO, K2, YO, K3, YO, K2: 19 sts.

Row 19: K2, YO, K5, YO, K1, slip 1 as if to knit, K2 tog, PSSO, K1, YO, K5, YO, K2: 21 sts.

Row 21: K2, YO, K7, YO, slip 1 as if to knit, K2 tog, PSSO, YO, K7, YO, K2: 23 sts.

Row 23: K2, YO, K1, † YO, K2, slip 1 as if to knit, K2 tog, PSSO, K2, YO †, K3, repeat from † to † once, K1, YO, K2: 25 sts.

Row 25: K2, YO, K3, † YO, K1, slip 1 as if to knit, K2 tog, PSSO, K1, YO †, K5, repeat from † to † once, K3, YO, K2: 27 sts.

Row 27: K2, YO, K5, YO, slip 1 as if to knit, K2 tog, PSSO, YO, K7, YO, slip 1 as if to knit, K2 tog, PSSO, YO, K5, YO, K2: 29 sts.

Row 29: K2, YO, K7, YO, K1, YO, K3, slip 1 as if to knit, K2 tog, PSSO, K3, YO, K1, YO, K7, YO, K2: 33 sts.

Row 30: K2, purl across to last 2 sts, K2.

Row 31: K2, YO, K1, ★ † YO, K2, slip 1 as if to knit, K2 tog, PSSO, K2, YO †, K3; repeat from ★ across to last 10 sts, repeat from † to † once, K1, YO, K2: 35 sts.

Row 33: K2, YO, K3, ★ † YO, K1, slip 1 as if to knit, K2 tog, PSSO, K1, YO †, K5; repeat from ★ across to last 10 sts, repeat from † to † once, K3, YO, K2: 37 sts.

Row 35: K2, YO, K5, ★ † YO, slip 1 as if to knit, K2 tog, PSSO, YO †, K7; repeat from ★ across to last 10 sts, repeat from † to † once, K5, YO, K2: 39 sts.

Row 37: K2, YO, K7, YO, K1, ★ YO, K3, slip 1 as if to knit, K2 tog, PSSO, K3, YO, K1; repeat from ★ across to last 9 sts, YO, K7, YO, K2: 43 sts.

Repeat Rows 30-37 until there are 11 complete leaf patterns down center of Body, ending by working Row 35.

Last 4 Rows: Knit across.

Bind off all sts in **knit**.

FRINGE

Holding 3 strands of fine weight yarn and 6 strands of super fine weight yarn together, each 10" (25.5 cm) long, add fringe to every other YO along both sides of Body and at center point (*Figs. 8a & b, page 20*).

pyramid shawl

Shown on page 15.

 **EASY +**

Finished Size: 53" wide x 26" long
(134.5 x 66 cm) excluding fringe

MATERIALS

Fine Weight Yarn
6 ounces, 170 grams
Super Fine Weight Yarn
3.5 ounces, 100 grams
29" (73.5 cm) Circular knitting needle,
size 10 (6 mm) **or** size needed for gauge
Crochet hook (for fringe)

GAUGE: In pattern, 18 sts = $4^3/4$" (12 cm)
and 36 rows = 5" (12.75 cm)

Techniques used:
*   YO *(Fig. 3, page 19)*
*   K2 tog *(Fig. 5, page 19)*
*   Slip 1 as if to knit, K2 tog, PSSO *(Figs. 6a & b, page 20)*
*   Slip 1 as if to knit, K1, PSSO *(Fig. 7, page 20)*

BODY

Holding 2 strands of super fine weight yarn and one strand of fine weight yarn together, cast on 20 sts.

Rows 1 and 2: Knit across.

Row 3 (Right side)**:** K2, YO, (K2 tog, YO) across to last 2 sts, K2: 21 sts.

Row 4 AND ALL WRONG SIDE ROWS: K2, purl across to last 2 sts, K2.

Row 5: K2, YO, K1, (YO, slip 1 as if to knit, K1, PSSO) 3 times, K3, (K2 tog, YO) 3 times, K1, YO, K2: 23 sts.

Row 7: K2, YO, K1, (YO, slip 1 as if to knit, K1, PSSO) 4 times, K1, (K2 tog, YO) 4 times, K1, YO, K2: 25 sts.

Row 9: K2, YO, K3, (YO, slip 1 as if to knit, K1, PSSO) 3 times, YO, slip 1 as if to knit, K2 tog, PSSO, YO, (K2 tog, YO) 3 times, K3, YO, K2: 27 sts.

Row 11: K2, YO, K5, (YO, slip 1 as if to knit, K1, PSSO) 3 times, K1, (K2 tog, YO) 3 times, K5, YO, K2: 29 sts.

Instructions continued on page 14.

Row 13: K2, YO, K7, (YO, slip 1 as if to knit, K1, PSSO) twice, YO, slip 1 as if to knit, K2 tog, PSSO, YO, (K2 tog, YO) twice, K7, YO, K2: 31 sts.

Row 15: K2, YO, K9, (YO, slip 1 as if to knit, K1, PSSO) twice, K1, (K2 tog, YO) twice, K9, YO, K2: 33 sts.

Row 17: K2, YO, K 11, YO, slip 1 as if to knit, K1, PSSO, YO, slip 1 as if to knit, K2 tog, PSSO, YO, K2 tog, YO, K 11, YO, K2: 35 sts.

Row 19: K2, YO, K 13, YO, slip 1 as if to knit, K1, PSSO, K1, K2 tog, YO, K 13, YO, K2: 37 sts.

Row 21: K2, YO, K 15, YO, slip 1 as if to knit, K2 tog, PSSO, YO, K 15, YO, K2: 39 sts.

Row 23: K2, YO, K1, † (YO, slip 1 as if to knit, K1, PSSO) 3 times, K3, (K2 tog, YO) 3 times †, K3, repeat from † to † once, K1, YO, K2: 41 sts.

Row 25: K2, YO, K1, ★ (YO, slip 1 as if to knit, K1, PSSO) 4 times, K1, (K2 tog, YO) 4 times, K1; repeat from ★ across to last 2 sts, YO, K2: 43 sts.

Row 27: K2, YO, K3, ★ (YO, slip 1 as if to knit, K1, PSSO) 3 times, YO, slip 1 as if to knit, K2 tog, PSSO, YO, (K2 tog, YO) 3 times, K3; repeat from ★ across to last 2 sts, YO, K2: 45 sts.

Row 29: K2, YO, K5, ★ (YO, slip 1 as if to knit, K1, PSSO) 3 times, K1, (K2 tog, YO) 3 times, K5; repeat from ★ across to last 2 sts, YO, K2: 47 sts.

Row 31: K2, YO, K7, ★ (YO, slip 1 as if to knit, K1, PSSO) twice, YO, slip 1 as if to knit, K2 tog, PSSO, YO, (K2 tog, YO) twice, K7; repeat from ★ across to last 2 sts, YO, K2: 49 sts.

Row 33: K2, YO, K9, ★ (YO, slip 1 as if to knit, K1, PSSO) twice, K1, (K2 tog, YO) twice, K9; repeat from ★ across to last 2 sts, YO, K2: 51 sts.

Row 35: K2, YO, K 11, ★ YO, slip 1 as if to knit, K1, PSSO, YO, slip 1 as if to knit, K2 tog, PSSO, YO, K2 tog, YO, K 11; repeat from ★ across to last 2 sts, YO, K2: 53 sts.

Row 37: K2, YO, K 13, ★ YO, slip 1 as if to knit, K1, PSSO, K1, K2 tog, YO, K 13; repeat from ★ across to last 2 sts, YO, K2: 55 sts.

Row 39: K2, YO, K 15, ★ YO, slip 1 as if to knit, K2 tog, PSSO, YO, K 15; repeat from ★ across to last 2 sts, YO, K2: 57 sts.

Row 41: K2, YO, K1, ★ † (YO, slip 1 as if to knit, K1, PSSO) 3 times, K3, (K2 tog, YO) 3 times †, K3; repeat from ★ across to last 18 sts, repeat from † to † once, K1, YO, K2: 59 sts.

Rows 42-183: Repeat Rows 24-41, 7 times; then repeat Rows 24-39 once **more**: 201 sts.

Rows 184 and 185: Knit across.

Bind off all sts in **knit**.

FRINGE

Holding 3 strands of fine weight yarn and 6 strands of super fine weight yarn together, each 10" (25.5 cm) long, add fringe in each YO along lower curved edge of Body and in every other YO along sides (*Figs. 8a & b, page 20*).

threaded
cover-up

 EASY

Finished Size: 23¹/₂" (59.5 cm) square, excluding tassles

MATERIALS

Bedspread Weight Cotton
Thread (size 10)
800 yards, 732 meters
29" (73.5 cm) Circular knitting needle,
size 1 (2.25 mm) **or** size needed for gauge

GAUGE: In pattern, 26 sts = 4" (10 cm)

Techniques used:
*   YO *(Fig. 3, page 19)*
*   K2 tog *(Fig. 5, page 19)*

BACK

Cast on 148 sts.

Row 1: K1, (YO, K2 tog) across to last st, K1.

Repeat Row 1 for pattern until piece measures approximately 7¹/₂" (19 cm) from cast on edge **or** to desired length.

NECK OPENING

Row 1: K1, (YO, K2 tog) 35 times, K1; with second ball, bind off next 4 sts for Neck opening, (YO, K2 tog) across to last st, K1: 72 sts **each** side.

Both sides of Neck Opening are worked at the same time, using a separate ball of thread for **each** side.

Row 2: K1, (YO, K2 tog) across to within one st of Neck opening, K1; with second ball, K1, (YO, K2 tog) across to last st, K1.

Repeat Row 2 for pattern until piece measures approximately 16" (40.5 cm) from cast on edge **or** to desired length.

FRONT

Row 1: K1, (YO, K2 tog) across to within one st of Neck opening, K1, **turn**; with same ball add on 4 sts *(Figs. 4a & b, page 19)*, **turn**; cut second ball, K1, (YO, K2 tog) across to last st, K1: 148 sts.

Row 2: K1, (YO, K2 tog) across to last st, K1.

Repeat Row 2 until Front measures same as Back.

Bind off all sts in **knit**.

TASSEL (Make 4)

Cut a piece of cardboard 3"
(7.5 cm) wide and the desired
length of the finished Tassel. Wind a
double strand of thread around the
cardboard approximately
20 times. Cut an 18" (45.5 cm)
length of thread and insert it
under the strands at the top of the
cardboard; pull up **tightly** and tie
securely. Leave the thread ends long
enough to attach the Tassel. Cut
the thread at the opposite end of
the cardboard *(Fig. A)* and then
remove it.

Wrap another length of thread
tightly around the Tassel twice,
$^1/_2$" (12 mm) below the top *(Fig. B)*;
tie securely then trim the ends.

Attach one Tassel to each corner of
Cover-up.

Fig. A

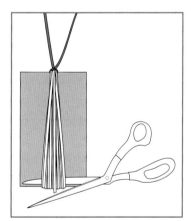

Fig. B

general instructions

ABBREVIATIONS

cm	centimeters
K	knit
mm	millimeters
P	purl
PSSO	pass slipped stitch over
Rnd(s)	Round(s)
st(s)	stitch(es)
tog	together
YO	yarn over

★ — work instructions following ★ as **many more** times as indicated in addition to the first time.

† to † — work all instructions from first † to second † **as many** times as specified.

( ) or [ ] — work enclosed instructions **as many** times as specified by the number immediately following **or** contains explanatory remarks.

colon (:) — the number(s) given after a colon at the end of a row or round denote(s) the number of stitches you should have on that row or round.

KNIT TERMINOLOGY

UNITED STATES		INTERNATIONAL
gauge	=	tension
bind off	=	cast off
yarn over (YO)	=	yarn forward (yfwd) **or** yarn around needle (yrn)

GAUGE

Exact gauge is essential for proper size. Before beginning your project, make a sample swatch in the yarn/thread and needles specified. After completing the swatch, measure it, counting your stitches and rows or rounds carefully. If your swatch is larger or smaller than specified, **make another, changing needle size to get the correct gauge**. Keep trying until you find the size needles that will give you the specified gauge. Once proper gauge is obtained, measure the width of the piece approximately every 3" (7.5 cm) to be sure gauge remains consistent.

Yarn Weight Symbol & Names	LACE 0	SUPER FINE 1	FINE 2	LIGHT 3	MEDIUM 4	BULKY 5	SUPER BULKY 6
Type of Yarns in Category	Fingering, size 10 crochet thread	Sock, Fingering, Baby	Sport, Baby	DK, Light Worsted	Worsted, Afghan, Aran	Chunky, Craft, Rug	Bulky, Roving
Knit Gauge Range* in Stockinette St to 4" (10 cm)	33-40** sts	27-32 sts	23-26 sts	21-24 sts	16-20 sts	12-15 sts	6-11 sts
Advised Needle Size Range	000-1	1 to 3	3 to 5	5 to 7	7 to 9	9 to 11	11 and larger

*GUIDELINES ONLY: The chart above reflects the most commonly used gauges and needle sizes for specific yarn categories.

** Lace weight yarns are usually knitted on larger needles to create lacy openwork patterns. Accordingly, a gauge range is difficult to determine. Always follow the gauge stated in your pattern.

◼◻◻◻ BEGINNER	Projects for first-time knitters using basic knit and purl stitches. Minimal shaping.
◼◼◻◻ EASY	Projects using basic stitches, repetitive stitch patterns, simple color changes, and simple shaping and finishing.
◼◼◼◻ INTERMEDIATE	Projects with a variety of stitches, such as basic cables and lace, simple intarsia, double-pointed needles and knitting in the round needle techniques, mid-level shaping and finishing.
◼◼◼◼ EXPERIENCED	Projects using advanced techniques and stitches, such as short rows, fair isle, more intricate intarsia, cables, lace patterns, and numerous color changes.

KNIT INCREASE

Knit the next stitch but do **not** slip the stitch off the left needle *(Fig. 1a)*. Insert the right needle into the back loop of the same stitch and knit it *(Fig. 1b)*, then slip the worked stitch off the left needle.

Fig. 1a

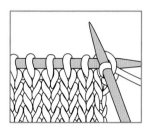

Fig. 1b

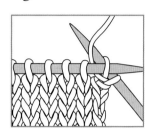

INVISIBLE INCREASE

Insert the right needle from the **front** into the side of the stitch **below** the next stitch on the left needle *(Fig. 2)* and knit it.

Fig. 2

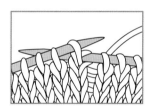

YARN OVER *(abbreviated YO)*

Bring the yarn forward **between** the needles, then back **over** the top of the right hand needle, so that it is now in position to knit the next stitch *(Fig. 3)*.

Fig. 3

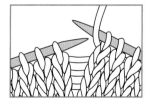

ADDING NEW STITCHES

Insert the right needle into the stitch as if to **knit**, yarn over and pull the loop through *(Fig. 4a)*. Insert the left needle into the loop just worked from **front** to **back** and slip the loop onto the left needle *(Fig. 4b)*. Repeat for the required number of stitches.

Fig. 4a

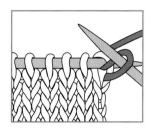

Fig. 4b

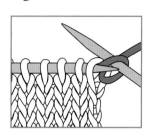

KNIT 2 TOGETHER
(abbreviated K2 tog)

Insert the right needle into the **front** of the first two stitches on the left needle as if to **knit** *(Fig. 5)*, then **knit** them together as if they were one stitch.

Fig. 5

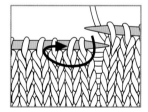

KNITTING NEEDLES																
U.S.	0	1	2	3	4	5	6	7	8	9	10	10½	11	13	15	17
U.K.	13	12	11	10	9	8	7	6	5	4	3	2	1	00	000	---
Metric - mm	2	2.25	2.75	3.25	3.5	3.75	4	4.5	5	5.5	6	6.5	8	9	10	12.75

SLIP 1, KNIT 2 TOGETHER, PASS SLIPPED STITCH OVER
(abbreviated slip 1, K2 tog, PSSO)
Slip one stitch as if to **knit** *(Fig. 6a)*, then K2 tog *(Fig. 5, page 19)*. With the left needle, bring the slipped stitch over the knit stitch *(Fig. 6b)* and off the needle.

Fig. 6a

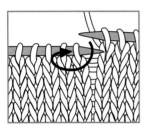

Fig. 6b

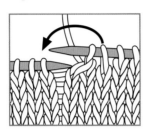

SLIP 1, KNIT 1, PASS SLIPPED STITCH OVER
(abbreviated slip 1, K1, PSSO)
Slip one stitch as if to **knit** *(Fig. 6a)*, then knit the next stitch. With the left needle, bring the slipped stitch over the knit stitch *(Fig. 7)* and off the needle.

Fig. 7

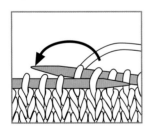

MARKERS
We have used a marker to indicate the beginning of rounds. Place the marker as instructed. You may use purchased markers or tie a length of contrasting color yarn around the needle. When you reach a marker on each round, slip it from the left needle to the right needle; remove it when no longer needed.

FRINGE
Cut a piece of cardboard 5" (12.5 cm) wide and half as long as the length of the strands indicated in the individual instructions. Wind the yarn **loosely** and evenly lengthwise around the cardboard until the card is filled, then cut across one end; repeat as needed.
Hold together the number of strands specified and fold in half.
With the **wrong** side facing and using a crochet hook, draw the folded end up through a stitch or space and pull the loose ends through the folded end *(Fig. 8a)*; draw the knot up **tightly** *(Fig. 8b)*. Repeat, spacing as specified in the individual instructions.
Lay piece flat on a hard surface and trim the ends.

Fig. 8a

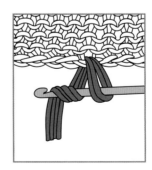

Fig. 8b

We have made every effort to ensure that these instructions are accurate and complete. We cannot, however, be responsible for human error, typographical mistakes, or variations in individual work.

Production Team: Instructional Writer/Editor - Lindsay White Glenn; Technical Editor - Lois J. Long; Editorial Writer - Susan McManus Johnson; Senior Graphic Artist - Lora Puls; Graphic Artist - Dana Vaughn; Photography Manager - Katherine Laughlin; Photo Stylist - Cora Holdaway; and Photographer - Jason Masters.